A Christmas Carol

Adapted by Dr. Andrew B. Harris

Scrooge

A Christmas Carol was first produced by the McKinney Repertory Theatre at the McKinney Performing Arts Center in November 2005. It was adapted, directed, and designed by Andrew Harris. The role of Dickens (Chad Lowe), Scrooge (Mel Tolle), Marley's Ghost (Jake Correll, who also served as the producer). The production has evolved and is now the "Annual Show." Musically, a violinist has replaced the original organist.

CAUTION: All rights whatsoever in this play are strictly reserved. Requests to reproduce the text in whole or in part should be addressed to the publisher.

Professional and Amateur Performing Rights: Applications for performance, including readings and excerpts, by professional and amateurs worldwide, should be addressed to the Author: Andrew Harris, ABH Productions Inc., 514 West Hunt Street, McKinney, Texas 75069. Tel. 011 (214) 876-9221.or email: andybharris@gmail.com
No performances of any kind may be made unless a license has been obtained. Applications should be made in advance of rehearsals commencing. Publication of this play does not necessarily indicate its availability. Mr. Harris is a Member of the Dramatists Guild of America.

Copyright © 2024 by Andrew B. Harris

Sentia Publishing Company has the exclusive rights to reproduce this work, to prepare derivative works from this work, to publicly distribute this work, to publicly perform this work, and to publicly display this work.

All rights reserved. No part of this publication may be reproduced, stored in a retrieval system, or transmitted, in any form or by any means, electronic, mechanical, photocopying, recording, or otherwise, without the prior written permission of the copyright owner.

Printed in the United States of America
ISBN 979-8-9915482-1-2

Dedicated to the memory of Doug Latham, the beloved director of MRT's production of *A Christmas Carol* who so lovingly dedicated his and his family's holiday season over the past several years to making each production of *A Christmas Carol* a memorable holiday tradition for *everyone* on and off stage. And to his wife, Marilyn Latham, who continues the family tradition by sharing Doug's vision and passion for the story. Finally, for everyone who has contributed their time and talents to MRT's production of *A Christmas Carol* over the years, "Thank you!"

A Christmas Carol by Charles Dickens

CHARLES DICKENS (1812–1870) was thirty-one years old and already the author of six major works including, Oliver Twist, The Pickwick Papers, and Nicolas Nickleby, when he was angered by a government report on the working conditions of children in Cornish tin mines in 1843. In October, he gave a speech in Manchester urging workers and employers to band together to control ignorance and champion educational reform. As a follow-up, Dickens had planned a pamphlet on the topic but eventually decided on a deeply felt imaginative work rather than a polemical essay. This approach allowed him to both reach people and vent his rage.

With pressure coming from his publisher due to lagging sales from his last book and with his wife pregnant with their fifth child, Dickens set about writing at a "white heat." During long walks, Dickens visualized fairy tale-like characters as contemporary Londoners. He completed the novella, A Christmas Carol, in six weeks—such a breakneck pace that the final lines in the story about Tiny Tim were not written until his book was already at press.

Dickens found it helpful to work with illustrators. George Cruikshank's work for sketches for Sketches by Boz (1836) and Oliver Twist (1838) were so dramatic that when Oliver Twist was staged at the Adelphi Theatre, the actors realized the scenes from the illustrations on stage. Specific moments in the action became tableaus, giving the audience the pleasure of seeing illustrations come to life, a technique that would become a staple in the motion picture industry. Unfortunately, Cruikshank was not available to illustrate A Christmas Carol, so John Leech got the job. To enhance his Christmas story, Dickens requested four hand-colored etchings and four black-and-white wood engravings, which Leech created for the first edition.

With an initial publishing run of just six thousand copies, A Christmas Carol sold out immediately, but the high cost of printing made additional publishing runs expensive, reducing the author's profit. Dickens, who earlier in life had wanted to be an actor, solved this problem by reading the work aloud on stage, and the novella rapidly gained popularity in this form. Staged adaptations by others followed, and the story began to influence the popular culture of the day. Dickens' ghost-filled story focused attention on the poor and disadvantaged, as the author had intended, but also made the phrase "Merry Christmas" an almost universal sentiment. In America, A Christmas Carol became Dickens' most popular work, selling over two million copies in its first one hundred years.

Twenty years ago, under Jake Correll's leadership, I was asked to direct To Kill a Mockingbird (Harper Lee, 1960), the first production in the newly renovated Courthouse, renamed the McKinney Performing Arts Center. The production was part of a joint effort by the Library and the McKinney Independent School District called "Read Across McKinney." Jake's nascent organization, called MRT (McKinney Repertory Theatre) gave the reading a theatrical twist. The setting for *Mockingbird*–in the Courtroom Theater– could not have been more appropriate, and reviewers loved it. The show played to packed houses.

Because one hit does not a theatre make, the success of *Mockingbird* prompted the question, "How can we top this?" *Mockingbird* was all about a child's-eye view of what was happening in a small southern town before the Civil Rights Era. Racial injustice was the background to an end of innocence story in which a child, Scout, the attorney's daughter, discovered that the neighbor she was most afraid of wasn't the person she really had to fear. Producing the play on stage required a community to come together, work together, and share a vision of a less divided world, where justice, not prejudice, reigned supreme.

It would be a tough act to follow, and we all knew it. Jake's suggestion for the season closer was *A Christmas Carol*. To do this, though, we would have to solve several problems. First, we did not have the rights to perform it. Secondly, we did not have enough time in the theatre to mount a nearly three-hour-long show. Finally, the Courtroom Theatre was only available for two days, and we needed to run the show at least four times. Drawing on my years of experience as an educator, director, and writer, I adapted an hour-long version of the play from the original novella and added music that was in the public domain. My emphasis, as with *Mockingbird*, was: "How can we build community?" I was fortunate to have cast members available from the previous show as well as students from my classes at the University of North Texas. With some changes and additions, *A Christmas Carol* has held the stage for nineteen years and continues to charm. It has developed a following among the cast, crew, and public. Hopefully, having it in print will enhance the experience.

Several of the illustrations that accompany this edition incorporate portions of 19th-century illustrated editions of the story. For the first production of our adaptation in 2005, I used portions of these 19th-century illustrations, which were painted onto canvas flats so that our actors appeared to be emerging from the pages of the novella. To reproduce something like that effect, we have decided to reuse those illustrations with members of the 2023 cast. We hope the experience of seeing Dickens' world populated with our performers recreates the thrill of a live production. Enjoy!

ABH

ACKNOWLEDGEMENTS

I wish to thank MRT and Dale Gutt, Artistic Director, and Davina Gazo Stampfel, Executive Director. Sarah Floyd, our Graphic Designer, for her inspiration and hard work. Assisting me at ABH Productions were Karen Dawkins, Michele Baker, Sandra Schulte, Madison Chapman, Joan Torres, Cheryl Craig, and Marilyn Latham. However, this whole project would not have happened were it not for the support of my wife Ann Harris and her enthusiasm. And finally, William England, our publisher, who came to see *A Christmas Carol* and who said, "Yes," one of the most powerful words in the world.

CHARACTERS

Cast in Order of Appearance:

Charles Dickens, author and narrator
Ebenezer Scrooge
Bob Cratchit, Scrooge's clerk
Gentleman 1
Gentleman 2
Fred, Scrooge's nephew, Fan's son
Woman on the Street
Jacob Marley, Scrooge's Partner
Ghost of Christmas Past
Young Scrooge
Little Fan, Scrooge's sister
Scrooge, as a Young Man
Belle
Fezziwig
Mrs. Fezziwig
Dick Wilkins, friend
Ghost of Christmas Present
Waifs (Want & Ignorance)
Mrs. Cratchit, Bob Cratchit's wife
Cratchit Children: Peter, Belinda, Natlie, Martha, Sally, Tiny Tim
Fred's Party: Mary (Fred's wife), Jack, Topper, Beth
Ghost of Christmas Future
Businessman 1
Businessman 2
Businessman 3
Businesswoman 1
Businesswoman 2
Old Joe
Undertaker's Boy
Mrs. Dilber
Mrs. Filcher
Boy in the Street

PLAY

(The VIOLINIST plays as the CAROLERS enter.)

[Tune Played: Oh Tannenbaum (sung in German)]

(The CAROLERS begin singing as the street goers walk through the crowd wishing them a Happy Holidays/Merry Christmas. As the carolers sing, the figure of DICKENS is observed sitting at a desk writing. (Dickens goes to the window and listens to the Carolers. Children Beggers enter, beg Carolers for money using their hats. One Caroler shews them away. Children run away and react with fear and hurt. They then run to the stairs by Scrooge's office. Dickens sees this happen.)

DICKENS
Now to just end the story. "And so as Tiny Tim observed, they lived happily ever after." No, that one is overdone. How about "And so as Tiny Tim observed, Bah Humbug! Smiley face." No that is probably ahead of its time. What I need is something simple and pure. I got it! I know just how to end it. *(Finishes writing the last sentence)* I do hope everyone will like it. I guess we will soon see. *(HE closes the book and looks at HIS watch)* Oh look at the time. I have places to go, people to see and things to do! I love Christmas!

(DICKENS stands, puts on his hat/scarf, and gloves, walks to the HL stairs and is met by BEGGAR 1.)

BEGGAR 1
Mr. Dickens, Mr. Dickens. A little help for the poor? And for the baby?

DICKENS
(handing BEGGAR 1 a coin) Certainly my good (man/woman).

(Dickens sees the children. He gives them coins. He puts his scarf around one child beggar and gives his gloves to the other. Mean Caroler comes in and walks across HR to HL. Dickens sees him.)

DICKENS

You there. Sir. Ignoring these children is no way to act at Christmas. These children are hungry and need provision.

> *(Caroler reacts with disdain at being called out, and continues to walk and exit HL door.)*

DICKENS

(*to* BEGGARS). Merry Christmas and God save you!

BEGGARS

Thank you, sir, and the same to you!

DICKENS

Come with me and let me tell you a wonderful story. *(Crosses to bench, opening the book)* Once upon a time…of all the good days in the year, on Christmas Eve…old Ebenezer Scrooge sat in his counting house.

> *(We begin to be aware of the hunched and pinched figure of Ebenezer Scrooge hovering over his desk)*

Scrooge had been partners for many years with Jacob Marley, so the firm was known as "Scrooge and Marley." Now, Marley was dead to begin with. There is no doubt whatsoever about that. Yes, old Marley was as dead as a doornail. Scrooge never painted out old Marley's name. There it stood years afterward above the door: "Scrooge and Marley."

> [Tune Played: Hark the Harold Angels Sing]
>
> *(The CAROLERS sing as the VIOLINIST plays)*

SCROOGE

(Banging the coal shovel) Stop that caterwauling! That's enough to wake the dead! Christmas. BAH Humbug!

> *(Lights up on DICKENS and the BEGGAR 1, DICKENS is reading from his book*

DICKENS

Oh, but that Scrooge was a tightfisted old miser. Hard and sharp as flint---a grasping, scraping, clutching, covetous, mean old sinner. And solitary as an oyster! Now Scrooge had a clerk named Bob Cratchit, and he paid the poor fellow, who had a wife and children, a salary that barely fed them.

(CRATCHIT lights SCROOGE's candle and then his own from the same match)

The place where Cratchit sat was like a dismal little cell.

(Lights down on DICKENS and the BEGGAR 1)

(We hear the sound of a quill pen scratching as CRATCHIT writes. He lays down the pen and rubs his hands together over the scant warmth of the candle on his desk. He gets up from his desk and goes to stove to warm his hands.)

SCROOGE

(looking up from his desk) Cratchit, get on with your work.

CRATCHIT

But it's cold and foggy sir. Penetrating.

SCROOGE

Cold? Nonsense! Haven't you a candle there on your desk?

CRATCHIT

Yes sir. But the figures suffer from my fingers being stiff.

SCROOGE

Warm your hands over the candle then. How many times must I tell you? I won't have my coal burned as if it were rubbish. If you insist on being so extravagant, we shall have to part company you and I. I can always find another clerk you know; more easily than you can find another position I warrant. Now back to work!

CRATCHIT
Yes sir.

(Cratchit returns to his desk. The office bell rings as two CHARITABLE GENTLEMEN enter.)

FIRST GENTLEMAN
Scrooge and Marley's, I believe. Have I the pleasure of addressing Mr. Scrooge or Mr. Marley?

SCROOGE
Mr. Marley has been dead these seven years. He died seven years ago– (*HE pauses*) seven years ago this very night.

FIRST GENTLEMAN
We have no doubt his generosity is well represented by his surviving partner.

(SCROOGE grunts noncommittally and returns to his work.)

SECOND GENTLEMAN
At this festive season of the year, Mr. Scrooge, it is more than usually desirable that we should make some slight provision for the poor and destitute, who suffer greatly at the present time.

(SCROOGE does not reply)
Many thousands are in want of common necessities. Hundreds of thousands are in want of common comforts, sir.

SCROOGE
Are there no prisons?

SECOND GENTLEMAN
Plenty of prisons.

SCROOGE
And the workhouses? Are they still in operation?

SECOND GENTLEMAN
They are. Still, I wish I could say they were not.

SCROOGE
The "treadmill" and the "Poor Law" are in full vigor, then?

SECOND GENTLEMAN
Both very busy sir.

SCROOGE
Good! I was afraid, from what you said at first, that something had happened to stop them in their useful course. I'm very glad to hear it.

FIRST GENTLEMAN
I'm sure you'll agree, sir, that they furnish but little cheer of mind or good to the multitude. Therefore, a few of us are endeavoring to raise a fund to buy the poor some meat and drink and means of warmth. (HE *gives* SCROOGE *a paper*) We choose this time because it is the time, above all others when abundance rejoices and want is keenly felt. What shall I put you down for?

SCROOGE
(*Letting the paper fall to the floor*)
Nothing!

FIRST GENTLEMAN
Ahh, you wish to remain anonymous?

SCROOGE
I wish to be left alone. Since you ask me what I wish, gentlemen, that is my answer. I don't make merry myself at Christmas, and I can't afford to make the idle people merry. If they wish to make merry, they must work as I do.

FIRST GENTLEMAN
Many can't find work.

SCROOGE
Well, then, my taxes support the establishments I have mentioned. They cost enough, and those who are badly off must go there.

SECOND GENTLEMAN

Many won't go there. Many would rather die.

SCROOGE

If they would rather die, they had better do so and decrease the surplus population. Besides, excuse me, but how do I know these things are true?

FIRST GENTLEMAN

But you must know it. You can't have shut your door on–

SCROOGE
(*Cutting him off*)

It is not my business! It's enough for a man to understand his own business and not to interfere with other people's. Mine occupies me constantly. Good afternoon, gentlemen.

(*Scrooge's nephew*, FRED, *enters as the two* CHARITABLE GENTLEMEN *are leaving the office area.*)

FRED

A Merry Christmas, uncle! God save you!

SCROOGE

Bah! Humbug!

FRED

Christmas a "humbug," uncle? You don't mean that, I'm sure.

SCROOGE

I do. "Merry Christmas!" What right have you to be *merry*? You're poor enough.

FRED

Come, then. What right have you to be dismal? You're *rich* enough.

SCROOGE

Bah! Humbug!

FRED

Don't be cross, uncle.

SCROOGE

What else can I be when I live in such a world of fools as this? What's Christmas time to you, but a time for paying bills without money; a time for finding yourself a year older and not an hour richer? If I could work my will every idiot, who goes about with "Merry Christmas" on his lips should be *boiled* in his own pudding with a stake of *holly* through his heart.

FRED

Uncle!

SCROOGE

Keep Christmas in your own way and let me keep it in mine.

FRED

But you don't keep it!

SCROOGE

Let me leave it alone, then. Much good may it do you. Much good it ever has done you!

FRED

There are many things from which I have derived good by which I have not profited—I dare say—Christmas among them. But I have always thought of Christmas time as a good time—a kind, forgiving, charitable, pleasant time. The only time in the long calendar of the year—when men and women seem by one consent—to open their shut-up hearts freely and remember that the people around them are really fellow passengers to the grave and not another race of creatures bound on other journeys. And, therefore, uncle—though it has never put a scrap of gold or silver into my pocket—I believe that it has done me *good* and will do me *good*—and I say, God bless it!

CRATCHIT
(Applauding)

Bravo!

SCROOGE
(*To* CRATCHIT)
Let me hear another sound from you, and ... you'll keep Christmas by losing your situation! (*To* FRED) There is another one—my clerk, with fifteen shillings a week and a wife and family—talking about a Merry Christmas. Bah!

FRED
Don't be angry, uncle. Come! Dine with us tomorrow.

SCROOGE
I'll see you– (HE *stops himself, then continues.*) I'll see you in hell first!

FRED
But why? Why?

SCROOGE
Why? Why did you marry against my wishes?

FRED
Why did I *marry*? Because i fell in love!

SCROOGE
"Because you fell in love!" If there is one thing in this world more ridiculous than "Merry Christmas," it is ... falling in love. Good afternoon!

FRED
I am sorry with all my heart to find you so resolute. But I have made this visit in homage to Christmas, and I'll keep my Christmas humor to the last. So, a Merry Christmas, uncle–

SCROOGE
Good afternoon!

FRED
And a happy New Year!

SCROOGE
Humbug! Good afternoon!

(FRED *exits. The clock chimes the hour.* CRATCHIT *scrambles as subtly as possible, preparing to leave.*)

CRATCHIT
(*Approaching* SCROOGE *hesitantly*)
Excuse me, sir, but it's–

SCROOGE
It's what?

CRATCHIT
It's closing time.

SCROOGE
Umh! You'll want all day tomorrow, I suppose?

CRATCHIT

If it's quite convenient, sir?

SCROOGE

It's <u>not</u> convenient, and it's not fair! If I were to dock you half a crown for it, you'd think yourself abused, wouldn't you? Yet, you don't think *me* abused when I pay a day's wages for <u>no</u> <u>work</u>?

CRATCHIT

It's only once a year.

SCROOGE

A poor excuse for picking a man's pocket every December the twenty-fifth. I suppose you must but ... be here all the earlier next morning..

CRATCHIT

Yes, sir (HE *starts to exit and turns.*) Merr–

>(CRATCHIT *breaks off and exits.* SCROOGE *has put on his shawl and hat.* HE *blows out his candle and closes the curtains.* HE *moves out of his office onto the street on his way home.*)

DICKENS

Meanwhile, the fog and darkness had thickened; the cold became intense—a piercing, searching, biting—cold. But external heat and cold had little influence on Scrooge. His own will had, for so long, removed him from feeling anything, that no warmth could warm him, nor wintry weather, chill him.

>(COUPLES *enter from the wings carrying lanterns and Christmas bundles and begin singing* "Life of Man" *in a round–the* MEN *first and then the* WOMEN. *The* SLED BOYS *take Cratchit's desk/sled around* SCROOGE *and then off.*)

COUPLES
(Singing)

The life of man is but a span

And cut down in its flower.
We're here today, tomorrow gone,
The creatures of an hour
Therefore, all good men be sure,
Wealth or rank possessing;
Ye who now will bless the poor
Shall yourselves find blessing

>(*The* COUPLES *move into scattered positions and* CRATCHIT *comes down with his sled and* THEY *sing the* "Wassail Song")

Now the winter bein' on us
And Christmas drawin' in
Please open your door
And let us come in
With our wassail

>(SCROOGE *continues on his way home encountering a* WOMAN, TWO BEGGAR GIRLS *and a* WOOD CARRIER.)

Wassail, wassail
And joy come to ye
Jolly wassail.

WOMAN
Merry Christmas–

SCROOGE
Bah!

WOMAN
Mr. Scrooge.

COUPLES
The master and mistress
Sittin' down at their ease

>(*The* TWO BEGGAR GIRLS *approach* SCROOGE *with tin cups.*)

SCROOGE
Away with you!

COUPLES
Put yer 'ands in yer pockets
And give what you please
With our wassail

(*The two* GIRLS *scurry off as a* WOOD CARRIER *enters with a load of wood.*)

WOOD CARRIER
(*Darkly*)
Merry Christmas, Mr. Scrooge.

COUPLES
Wassail, wassail
And joy come to ye
Jolly wassail

(*There is a pause as the* WOOD CARRIER *passes.* SCROOGE *continues of the way, muttering to himself. We hear the loneliness music again, faintly.* DICKENS *and* SCROOGE *walk toward each other along a wall which the people in the street have formed. As* DICKENS *narrates,* SCROOGE *continues feeling his way along the wall of flesh.*)

DICKENS
Scrooge had taken his usual melancholy dinner in his usual melancholy tavern and was on his way home to bed. He lived in chambers that had once belonged to his deceased partner. It was old now, and dreary, for nobody lived in it anymore but Scrooge. The yard was so dark that even Scrooge, who knew its every stone, was fain to grope with his hands. But darkness is cheap, so he liked it, the old miser, and gradually he made his way to the door. I will leave it to you to explain how it happened that Scrooge, having his key in the lock of the door, saw in the knocker not a knocker but the face of his dead partner, Jacob Marley.

(DICKENS *produces a death-mask likeness of Marley's face and holds it up, mirror-like, before* SCROOGE, *who now stands face to face with Marley, with death itself.* SCROOGE *recoils and the apparition disappears.*)

SCROOGE

Uh! (*Recovering*) Bah! Humbug! Rubbish! Nothing to it.

DICKENS

He turned the key and, as if unlocking some secret chamber of the spirit within him where long-forgotten dreams are hidden, he crossed the threshold and went inside.

(DICKENS *vanishes. As* SCROOGE *enters the house,. The strange music and echoing of its innards drift around him.* HE *examines his rooms.*)

SCROOGE

Nobody in the cupboard. Nobody under the bed. Nobody behind the curtains. Nobody here at all.

>*(After surprising his dressing gown as if it were a suspicious intruder,* HE *then slowly goes to the fire and sits down. A bell, somewhere high above, begins to ring, joining the other music which has been building throughout the scene. It now takes on a very ominous quality. The bell is joined by dragging chains, hollow groans, and other sounds. As they build, the fettered figure of* MARLEY'S GHOST *begins to appear, as if extricating himself from the wall.* SCROOGE *cries out to it, as if* HE *could will the Apparition to disappear.)*

SCROOGE

Humbug! Humbug! How now! What do you want with me?

MARLEY

Much!

SCROOGE

Who are you?

MARLEY

In life, I was your partner, Jacob Marley.

SCROOGE

Can you–can you sit down?

MARLEY

I can.

SCROOGE

Do it, then.

MARLEY

Do you believe in me?

SCROOGE
I don't.

MARLEY
What evidence would you have of my reality beyond that of your own senses? Why do you doubt me then?

SCROOGE
Because little things affect the senses. A slight disorder of the stomach can deceive them. For all I know, you may be an undigested bit of beef, a blot of mustard, a crumb of cheese, or a fragment of an underdone potato. There's more gravy than grave about you, whatever you are!
    (MARLEY *raises a cry*)
Mercy! Dreadful apparition, why do you trouble me?

MARLEY
O man of the worldly mind! Do you believe in me or not?

SCROOGE
I do, I do, I do. I must. But Spirit, why do you walk the earth, and why do you come to me?

MARLEY

It is required of every man that the spirit within him should walk abroad among his fellow men, and travel far and wide. And if that spirit goes not forth in life it is condemned to do so after death. It is doomed to wander through the world and witness what it cannot share but might have shared on earth and turned into happiness. (HE *raises another cry*.)

SCROOGE

You are chained and fettered. Tell me why.

MARLEY

I wear the chains I forged in life. I made them, link by link and yard by yard. Is their pattern strange to you? I tell you, the foil you bear yourself was as heavy and as long as this seven Christmas Eves ago. You have labored on it since. It is a ponderous chain.

SCROOGE

Old Jacob Marley–speak comfort to me, Jacob.

MARLEY

I have none to give. Comfort is conveyed by other ministers to other kinds of men. Mark me! In life, my spirit never roved beyond the narrow limits of our money-changing hole. Now I cannot rest, I cannot stay, I cannot linger anywhere. O, blind man! Blind man! Not to see that this earth is ever advancing toward a state of light! Not to know that each mortal life, however brief or small its sphere, has the power to bring us one step nearer that perfection. Not to understand that no amount of regret can make amends for one life's opportunities misused! Yet such was I. O, such was I!

SCROOGE

But you were always a good man of business, Jacob.

MARLEY

Business! Mankind was my business. Charity, mercy, and benevolence were all, all my business. The dealings of my trade were but a drop of water in the comprehensive ocean of my business. Hear me! My time is almost gone. I have come tonight to give you one last hope of escaping my fate.

SCROOGE
One last hope! You were always a good friend to me Jacob. Thank'ee

MARLEY
You will be haunted by three spirits.

SCROOGE
Is that the hope you mentioned, Jacob?

MARLEY
It is.

SCROOGE
I–I think I'd rather not.

MARLEY
Without their visits, you cannot hope to shun the path I tread. Expect the first tonight, when the bell tolls one. Expect the second on the next hour, when the bell tolls two.

SCROOGE
Couldn't I see 'em all at once and get it over with?

MARLEY
And the third upon the next tolling, at the hour of three. Look to see me no more—and look that, for your own sake that you remember what has passed between us!

> (MARLEY'S *ghost dissolves back into the wall amid a chorus of laments and wails emanating from the darkness, while the bell tolls midnight.*)

SCROOGE
Hum–

> (HE *slowly collapses onto* his bed and falls fast asleep. HE *wakes with a start. The sound of clockworks grinding, and disturbed underscores the following.* SCROOGE *looks at his pocket watch*)

Twelve o'clock! Why it must have been past two when I fell asleep. What does the tower clock say? Twelve! An icicle must have gotten into the clockworks. Twelve! Is it possible that something has happened to the sun, and it is twelve o'clock noon? Expect the first when the bell tolls one!

    (*The quarter-hour rings*)

A quarter past!

    (*The half-hour rings*)

Half past!

    (*The quarter-hour rings*)

A quarter to it!

    (*The clock strikes one*)

One o'clock! The hour itself—and nothing else. I knew it!

    (*The music and embodiment of the* GHOST OF CHRISTMAS PAST *and* HIS FAMILY, *dressed in the faded finery of the late 18th Century, the time of* SCROOGE'S *youth, begin to invade the room. The* CHILDREN *pull a sled bearing a decorated Christmas tree, dusty and faded. The* WIFE *carries an ice-covered branch*)

Are you the spirit, sir, whose coming was foretold to me:

    CHRISTMAS PAST

I am!

    SCROOGE

Who, and what, are you?

    CHRISTMAS PAST
    (*Laughing gently with other* SPIRITS)

I am the Ghost of Christmas Past.

    SCROOGE

Long past?

CHRISTMAS PAST
(THEY *laugh again*.)

No, your past.

SCROOGE

What brings you here?

CHRISTMAS PAST

Your welfare.

SCROOGE

I'm much obliged to you for rousing me in the dead of night to discuss my welfare.

CHRISTMAS PAST

Your reclamation, then. You know that I was there so long ago, your spirit friend unseen. I sparked the candles on your first green tree.

(*Filled with wonder,* SCROOGE *examines HIS first childhood Christmas tree.*)

I saw a light then, clear and pure, shining in your fresh new eyes. How dim it has become! Take heed! Rise with me and ride the night wind.

SCROOGE
But I am mortal and liable to fall.

CHRISTMAS PAST
Bear but a touch of my hand there, and you shall be upheld in more than this.

SCROOGE
O heavens, I was born in this place. I was a boy here.

(*Five* HORSEBOYS *enter* UR *on stick horses swinging bird sticks rhythmically over their heads. They sing with accompaniment.*)

HORSEBOYS
(*Singing*)
Twenty red horses on a white hill
Now they run, now they jump
Now they stand still

SCROOGE
There's Jim, Pip, Davy, Clive, Frank.

HORSEBOYS
Twenty red horses on a white hill
Now they run, now they jump
Now they stand still

SCROOGE
O Jim, Pip, Davy, Clive, and Frank.

HORSEBOYS
Twenty red horses on a white hill
Now they run, now they jump
Now they stand still

(*The* HORSEBOYS *have formed a line in front of what is to become the schoolroom.*)

CHRISTMAS PAST
They are but shadows of things that once were. They have no consciousness of us.

SCROOGE
Why, this is the old river road!

CHRISTMAS PAST
You remember the way?

SCROOGE
Remember it! I could walk it blindfolded.

CHRISTMAS PAST
Yet you have forgotten it for so long.

SCROOGE
I remember it all–the old oak tree, that rusty iron gate, and there's the school! The boys have all gone home for their Christmas Holidays.

CHRISTMAS PAST
The old school is not quite deserted. A solitary child, abandoned by his friends, is left there still.

SCROOGE
I know.

(BOY SCROOGE *is alone at his seat*)
Poor lonely boy ...

BOY SCROOGE
(*Reading aloud from the first chapter of* Robinson Crusoe.)

Robinson Crusoe by Daniel Defoe. "I was born in the year 1632 in the city of York..."

(*Then a little girl appears as if* SCROOGE *had wished her out of the past.* LITTLE FAN *carefully comes up behind* BOY SCROOGE *to surprise him.*)

SCROOGE
Little Fan!

LITTLE FAN
Dear, dear Ebenezer!

BOY SCROOGE
Dear sister!

LITTLE FAN
I came to bring you home, dear brother. To bring you home, home, home!

BOY SCROOGE
Home, Little Fan?

LITTLE FAN
Yes. Home for good! Home forever! Poor brother. Father was always so cruel to you, but now he's so much kinder–that home's like heaven. I'd never even dared to say your name, but one night he spoke to me so gently, that I just had to ask him once more if you might come home for Christmas. And do you know what he said? He said, "Yes," and he sent me to bring you. You are never to come back here again. We'll be together all Christmas long and have the merriest time in all the world!

BOY SCROOGE
You are quite a woman, Little Fan.

(THEY *prepare to depart.*)

SCROOGE
(*Reaching out as if attempting to touch his boyhood self.*)
Where has he gone–that other me, that little child, myself–myself as I used to be?

CHRISTMAS PAST

She was always a delicate creature whom a breath might have withered, but she had a great heart.

SCROOGE

So, she had. You're right; I'll not deny it. Spirit.

CHRISTMAS PAST

She died a woman and had, I believe, children.

SCROOGE

Only one child.

CHRISTMAS PAST

True, your nephew, Fred. She died when he was born.

SCROOGE

Yes, I remember.

CHRISTMAS PAST

As your mother died when you were born.

SCROOGE

I know.

CHRISTMAS PAST

So, you turned away from him… (SCROOGE *doesn't answer*.) …as your father turned away from you..

(*The voice of the* CAROLER *echoes over the scene as* LITTLE FAN *and* BOY SCROOGE *exit together, singing the* CAROLER'S *song*.)

SCROOGE

I wish…but it's too late now.

CHRISTMAS PAST

What is it?

SCROOGE

Nothing ...

CHRISTMAS PAST

Something ...

SCROOGE

Nothing ... There was a boy singing a Christmas carol at my window last night. I should like to have given him something, that's all.

CHRISTMAS PAST

Come; we have other Christmases to see.

>(*Evening descends on the scene, and the stage is turned to ice.* CHRISTMAS PAST'S CHILDREN *pull on the empty sled to suggest the new scene.* BELLE COUSINS, *skating alone on the frozen pond, glides onto the stage and calls out to the* YOUNG SCROOGE *to follow her.*)

BELLE

Ebenezer!

SCROOGE

Belle!

>(YOUNG SCROOGE *glides on to join* BELLE, *and they skate together.*)

BELLE
(*Stopping*)
O look, Ebenezer–The first star!

YOUNG SCROOGE
(*Looking up*)
Where?

BELLE

Look. See? (SHE *points*) Over the steeple there.

YOUNG SCROOGE

Oh, yes. It's so bright.

BELLE

The first one always seems the brightest.

YOUNG SCROOGE

Mmmmm ...

BELLE

Did you make a wish?

YOUNG SCROOGE

A wish?

BELLE

Yes! A wish upon a star.

YOUNG SCROOGE

No. Did you?

BELLE

Of course. And you should, too. Especially tonight. They say the first star on Christmas night is the most magical one of the whole year.

YOUNG SCROOGE

All right.

(*There is a pause as he skates.*)

BELLE

What is it?

YOUNG SCROOGE

What's what?

BELLE

Your wish?

YOUNG SCROOGE

Is it all right to tell?

BELLE

Well, you're not supposed to, but if you don't tell me, you'll go away tomorrow, and I'll wonder about it all year long ... Tell me.

YOUNG SCROOGE

I wish ...

BELLE

Go on.

YOUNG SCROOGE

I wish I were part of the world, part of the real world, and someday make a fortune all my own. I wish that when I get to London, I am apprenticed to some great man of business. In time, I will advance to a high position in the firm. I'll be right up there with men of wealth and power. Just think of it!... What did you wish?

BELLE
I wish you wouldn't go.

YOUNG SCROOGE
Oh, Belle ...

BELLE
I'll miss you so.

YOUNG SCROOGE
You know I'll miss you, too. It won't be for long. You'll see. But I must go.

BELLE
I know you must, but I don't know why.

YOUNG SCROOGE
I need to prove myself to…

BELLE
To whom? Not to me. You know that in my heart, you will always be the highest and the best.

YOUNG SCROOGE
It isn't that…Oh, Belle, you have that noble quality of gentle hearts. You see only the good… it's not to you…

BELLE
To whom, then? To your father?

YOUNG SCROOGE
No! He doesn't even know I'm alive. I'm sure he will never mention my name again, except in a drunken reproach. Let him, if he pleases. What do I care? For me, he no longer exists. He might as well be dead!

BELLE
I believe it is your father. You've never forgotten his cruelty.

YOUNG SCROOGE
Yes, I have forgotten! I've forgotten my father. I've forgotten I ever was a child. I only remember the cold, the endless hours of work, the beatings—I've had enough of doing porter's work, of holding horses in the streets and never having a farthing to call my own. I will never be free to love you until I have buried all that completely.

BELLE
You will never be able to bury him, Ebenezer. If you could only temper your bitterness toward him, you would free your heart. If you would but sometimes, in some quiet hour, beside the winter fire or in the summer air when you hear gentle music, think of home and childhood, resolve to look with true compassion on him or anyone who ever wronged you, I know you would forgive him in your heart.

YOUNG SCROOGE
Ah, Belle! You are a treasure beyond all price.

BELLE
Look! Now the sky is filled with stars!

YOUNG SCROOGE
You have my promise to return to you a better man than he who says farewell.

BELLE
And I promise to wait for you.

(Scrooge blows a kiss to Belle and gives her the star trinket.)

SCROOGE
She was an angel!

CHRISTMAS PAST
That heart where self has found. No home is slow to recognize its hungry face in others.

SCROOGE

: I wanted to give her the world.

CHRISTMAS PAST

Are you quite sure that is what she wanted? Listen!

(*The voice of* FEZZIWIG *is heard, as if echoing down a long corridor.*)

FEZZIWIG
(*From off stage*)

Yo ho, there!

CHRISTMAS PAST

I hear another Christmas calling to us.

FEZZIWIG
(*Off stage, approaching*)

Halloooo! Hallooo! Yo ho, there Dick! Ebenezer!

(CHRISTMAS PAST *and* HIS FAMILY *arrange the scene to suggest Fezziwig's warehouse.* FEZZIWIG *approaches trippingly. As* FEZZIWIG *appears.*)

SCROOGE

Why, It's old Fezziwig! Bless his heart, it's old Fezziwig alive again!

CHRISTMAS PAST

You know this place?

SCROOGE

Know it! Why, it's old Fezziwig's warehouse. I was apprenticed here.

FEZZIWIG

Yo ho! Dick! Ebenezer!

(DICK WILKINS *enters, finishing up his work.*)

SCROOGE

Why, it's Dick Wilkins, to be sure! Bless me, yes; there he is. Dear Dick!

(YOUNG SCROOGE *enters*)
And there's myself.

FEZZIWIG
Yo ho, my boys! No more work tonight! Christmas Eve, Dick. Christmas Eve Ebenezer. Let's have the shutters up, lads.

WILKINS
Quicker than you can say "Jack Robinson!"

FEZZIWIG
Let's clear away here.

YOUNG SCROOGE
As good as done, sir.

FEZZIWIG
Hilli-ho! Let's have lots of room here! Hilli-ho, Dick Chirrup, Ebenezer!

(MRS. FEZZIWIG *drifts in with her "one vast substantial smile."*)

Mrs. Fezziwig!

(THEY *embrace*.)

Just look at you, m' dear. All aglow. (*Assuming a Shakespearean stance.*) "Shining like a good deed in a naughty world" Will you deign to be my partner?

MRS. FEZZIWIG
Why, Mr. Fezziwig, I'd be delighted! If you think me worthy.

FEZZIWIG
You are worthy to be my partner in every sense of the word! You are worthy to be a king's partner, my love. If that's not high praise, tell me higher, and I'll use it!

MRS. FEZZIWIG
Very well, then let's foot it! The floor's swept and watered, the lamps are trimmed, fuel's on the fire. It's as snug and warm and bright a ballroom as you could desire to see on a winter's night!

(*The* FEZZIWIG GUESTS *begin to drift on in dance. The dance builds until it finally collapses as* DICK WILKINS *falls.*)

FEZZIWIG

Well done!

MRS. FEZZIWIG

Well done indeed!

FEZZIWIG

I can see we've got our work cut out for us tonight m'dear.

MRS. FEZZIWIG

I think we'll be a match for 'em.

(*The* FEZZIWIGS *lead a second dance, even livelier than the first–and, this time more successful. The dance finishes with a flourish. The clock begins sounding eleven. Couples start to disperse to their homes, wishing one and all a Merry Christmas as they begin to vanish into the night. By the time the last note has finished vibrating, The* FEZZIWIGS a*re left alone with* DICK WILKINS *and* YOUNG SCROOGE.)

MRS. FEZZIWIG

Oh, I hate to see the party end, it was such a wonderful evening. Wonderful dancing. Wonderful friends!

FEZZIWIG

All the world is wonderful at Christmas time.

CHRISTMAS PAST
(*to Scrooge*)

Wasn't Fezziwig a foolish man?

SCROOGE

A foolish man? No, no! He was a marvelous chap, a splendid fellow! The kindest man I ever knew.

CHRISTMAS PAST

He has spent but a few pounds of your mortal money. Is that so much that he deserves this praise?

SCROOGE

It isn't that ... (HIS *voice is suspended as if searching for the next word.*)

FEZZIWIG

Good night, Dick! Good night, Ebenezer! Here you go!

(FEZZIWIG *gives a little present to each.*)
A Merry Christmas to you, lads.

WILKINS
A Merry Christmas to you, sir! Merry Christmas Mrs. Fezziwig.

YOUNG SCROOGE
Merry Christmas!

MRS. FEZZIWIG
Merry Christmas–and pleasant dreams.

FEZZIWIG
Tomorrow's all yours, lads! Sleep as late as you will. Now off you go!

(YOUNG SCROOGE *and* DICK WILKINS *exit.*)
Mrs. Fezziwig, shall we?

(*The* FEZZIWIGS *go off together, arm in arm.*)

SCROOGE
He had the power to render us happy or unhappy, to make our service a pleasure or a toil. The happiness he gave was quite as great as if it cost a fortune…I wish… (HIS *voice trails off.*)

CHRISTMAS PAST
What's the matter?

SCROOGE
Nothing particular.

CHRISTMAS PAST
Something, I think.

SCROOGE
No, no … I should like to say a word or two to my own clerk, Bob Cratchit, just now, that's all.

CHRISTMAS PAST
My time grows short. Another Christmas is already hard upon us.

(CHRISTMAS PAST'S FAMILY *moves the sled bearing the Christmas tree into place for the next scene.* BELLE *enters and begins to un-trim the tree, continuing to do so throughout the scene.* YOUNG SCROOGE *follows her on a moment later.*)

YOUNG SCROOGE

Belle, please. You must believe me. This matters a great deal to me!

BELLE

Matters little to you. Very little. Another idol has displaced me. If it can comfort you in time to come, as I would have done. I have no cause to grieve.

YOUNG SCROOGE

What idol has displaced you?

BELLE

A golden one

YOUNG SCROOGE

Oh, I see. (*After a pause*) There is nothing the world hates more than poverty–yet nothing it professes to hate more than the pursuit of wealth!

BELLE

You fear the world too much. All your dreams you've locked away, beyond the world's reproach. I have seen your nobler aspirations shut away. I've watched your tenderest emotions wither, one by one–until the master passion, greed, possesses you.

YOUNG SCROOGE

What of that? I have grown wiser in the ways of the world, that is all. But I have not changed toward you. Have I? Have I?

BELLE

The promise we share is now an old one. It was made when we were both poor; and I, for one, was content to be so. Now you are changed. When it was made, you were another man.

YOUNG SCROOGE

I was a boy.

BELLE

You know in your heart that you are not what you were. How often I have thought of this, I cannot say. It is enough that I have thought of it and can release you.

YOUNG SCROOGE

Have I ever sought a release?

BELLE

In words? No. Never.

YOUNG SCROOGE

In what, then?

BELLE

In a changed nature. In an altered spirit. In everything that made my love of any value in your sight. If we have never made that promise to each other, tell me; would you seek me out and try to win me now? Ah, no…

YOUNG SCROOGE

You think not.

BELLE

I would gladly think otherwise if I could, heaven knows! But if you were free today, can I believe that you would choose a girl without a dowry? You, who weigh everything by profit? I cannot–and I release you, with a full heart, for the love of him you once were.

(SHE *starts to hand* HIM *the star. But it falls to the floor between them and shatters.*)

My memories almost make me hope our parting will cause you pain. It will be very brief, for you will bury the recollection of it gladly, as another unprofitable dream. May you be happy in the life you have chosen.

(YOUNG SCROOGE *is left alone as* BELLE *exits from his life forever.* HE *picks up the shattered star.*)

YOUNG SCROOGE
(*Crying out*)
Belle!

SCROOGE
(*To* YOUNG SCROOGE *as he starts to exit.*)
Fool! You could have stopped her!

CHRISTMAS PAST
She might have been a springtime in the haggard winter of your life.

SCROOGE
Spirit, show me no more! Conduct me home. Why do you delight in torturing me?

CHRISTMAS PAST
There is but one shadow more.

SCROOGE
No more. No. No. No more! I don't wish to see it! Show me no more!

CHRISTMAS PAST
I told you these were shadows of things that have been.

SCROOGE
I cannot bear it! Leave me! Show me no more! Haunt me no longer!

(SCROOGE *finds himself near his bed and collapses into a heavy sleep. A tone of peace settle on the stage. The bell tolls two.*)

DICKENS
He turned upon the Ghost and wrestled with it. But the Ghost gave no visible means of resistance and Scrooge became conscious only of being exhausted. Overcome by drowsiness, and finding himself in his own bed, he sank into a heavy sleep. He awoke to find a jolly Giant, who bore a glowing torch, holding it up high, shedding light upon him as he came peeping out from under the covers.

(CHRISTMAS PRESENT *enters with a torch glowing and a big smile.*)

CHRISTMAS PRESENT

Come out! Come up, and know me better, man! I am the Ghost of Christmas Present. Look upon me! You have never seen the like of me before?

SCROOGE

Never!

CHRISTMAS PRESENT

Have you never met my brothers?

SCROOGE

I don't think I have. I am afraid I have not. Have you many brothers, spirit?

CHRISTMAS PRESENT

More than eighteen hundred.

SCROOGE

A tremendous family to provide for!

CHRISTMAS PRESENT

Are you ready?

SCROOGE

Spirit, conduct me where you will. Tonight, if you will lead me, I will follow.

CHRISTMAS PRESENT

Take my staff.

(HE *hands* SCROOGE *his staff. The Crachit dining room begins to come to life. The* CRATCHIT CHILDREN *carry on a table. Chattering among themselves, the* CHILDREN *set the table and bring on the chairs.*)

NED
(*As* MRS. CRATCHIT *enters*)
Mother! Mother! Outside the Baker's we smelled the goose.

MRS. CRATCHIT
How do you know it's ours?

SALLY
It must be ours! It must be ours!

NED
Sage and onion. Sage and onion.

SALLY
Ooohh, Peter, how beautiful you look in Papa's collar!

MRS. CRATCHIT
Now, let Peter alone. (*Straightening his collar.*) He looks very handsome and very grown up. (*To Belinda*) Go and see if your father's coming. (*To the others*) What can be keeping your precious father, then? And your brother, Tiny Tim? And Martha wasn't as late last Christmas Day by half an hour.

BELINDA
Here's Martha, Mother!

(MARTHA *enters.*)

NED & SALLY
Here's Martha, Mother! Hurrah!

MRS. CRATCHIT
Why, bless your heart alive, my dear, how late you are!

NED
There's such a goose, Martha.

MARTHA
Oh, you never would believe what a deal of work we had to finish up last night. And then we had to clear it all away this morning.

MRS. CRATCHIT

Well, never mind, so long as you're here. Sit ye down before the fire and have warm. Oh, your hands are like ice! I'm so happy you're home. Lord bless ye!

BELINDA

No, No! There's Father coming.

NED & SALLY

Hide, Martha, hide!

(MARTHA *hides as* CRATCHIT *enters with* TINY TIM *on his shoulder.*)

CHILDREN

Papa! Papa!

(*The* CHILDREN *go to him*)

NED

Tiny Tim, we went past the Baker's where our goose is roasting!

SALLY

We smelled our goose! We smelled our goose!

CRATCHIT

Why, where's our Martha, then?

MRS. CRATCHIT

Not coming.

CRATCHIT

Not coming! Not coming home on Christmas Day?!

(*The* CHILDREN *have formed a line in front of* MARTHA.)

TINY TIM

There she is!

MARTHA

Oh, Father, Merry Christmas!

SALLY

Come, Tiny Tim! Come and hear the pudding siging in the copper.

NED & SALLY

Come on Tiny Tim!

MRS. CRATCHIT

Now, children–such excitement! Let him have a warm by the fire. Go with Peter.

PETER

Come with me to get the goose!

NED & SALLY

The goose! The goose!

(THEY *exit with* PETER)

MRS. CRATCHIT
(*To* CRATCHIT)

Well, how did Tiny Tim behave?

CRATCHIT

As good as gold and better. He must grow thoughtful, sitting by himself so much of the time. He says the strangest things you've ever heard. He told me coming home –what was that you told me, Tiny Tim, on the way home, about the people in church?

TINY TIM

I hoped the people saw me in church. Because it might be good to remember on Christmas Day who made the lame to walk and the blind to see.

(CRATCHIT *and* MRS. CRATCHIT *look at each other.*)

CRATCHIT

He's growing so strong and healthy.

(PETER, NED, and SALLY enter with the goose, to hurrahs and fanfares from all quarters. Everyone descends on the table and prepares for the feast.)

There never was such a goose! A Merry Christmas to us all, my dears. God Bless us.

(ALL repeat "God bless us" at random.)

TINY TIM
(After the others have spoken)

God bless us, everyone.

PETER

Three cheers for Tiny Tim!

ALL

Hip, hip, hooray! Hip, hip, hooray! Hip, hip, hooray!

(The cheers gradually fade in volume, and the lights on the CRATCHIT table dim as SCROOGE comes near it.)

SCROOGE

Spirit, tell me, will Tiny Tim live?

CHRISTMAS PRESENT

I see a vacant seat in the poor chimney corner and a crutch without an owner. If these shadows remain unaltered by the future, the boy will die.

SCROOGE

No, No! Oh, no, kind spirit! Say he will be spared.

CHRISTMAS PRESENT

If he be like to die, what then? He had better do it and, "decrease the surplus population."

(SCROOGE bows his head.)
Will you decide what men shall live, what men shall die?

(As the lights come up on it, the CRATCHIT table, they come up on FRED's parlor, with laughter and merriment

ringing through the transition to the next scene. FRED, MARY, *and* THEIR GUESTs *are in the midst of a game of "Blindman's Bluff." * FRED *is "it" and enjoying it immensely.*)

SCROOGE
Who's that? Why, it's my nephew, Fred!

(FRED *catching* MARY *and identifying her by her shape and clothes, causing her to giggle.*)

FRED
Aha! What could this be wrapped up in all these Christmas trimmings? (*Exploring with his hands.*) Beth? Meg? Topper? *(*FRED *laughs)* Why, bless me, it's my own dear Mary!

MARY
All right, now Fred. Let's play something peaceful.

JACK
Why not a game of "Yes and No"?

TOPPER
But how do you play it?

BETH
Well, "Fred, say, must think of something, and it's up to the rest of us to find out what!

MEG
But you can only answer "yes" or "no."

FRED
Very well. I've got one.

TED
Is it a vegetable?

       FRED
No.

       JACK
Animal, then?

       FRED
Yes.

       TED
A *live* animal?

       FRED
Yes.

       MARY
Would you have one for a pet?

       FRED
Noooo.

       MEG
Oh! It must be a rather disagreeable animal.

       FRED
Yes.

       BETH
A savage animal?

       FRED
Yes.

       JACK
Does it growl?

       FRED
Yes.

       TOPPER
     (*As a joke*)

Does it talk?

FRED
Yes

(There is general puzzlement over the fact that it talks.)
Sometimes.

ALL
Sometimes?

BETH
How many legs does it have?

MEG
Beth, only "yes and "no" questions.

BETH
Sorry!

TOPPER
Is it a bear?

FRED
No.

JACK
Does it live on a farm?

FRED
No.

TOPPER
Well, where does it live then? In London?

FRED
Yes!

TED
Does it walk the streets?

FRED

Yes!

MARY

Is it in a show?

BETH

I've found it out! I know what it is, Fred. I know what it is!

FRED

What is it?

BETH

It is your Uncle Scrooge!

FRED

It certainly is!

TOPPER
(*In joking protest*)

I say now! I object! When we asked if it was a bear, the answer should have been "yes!"

FRED
(*Enjoying his joke*)

Oh, well, he's a comical old fellow; that's the truth. And not so pleasant as he might be, God knows. But his offenses carry their own punishment.

MARY

But he's very rich, Fred. At least you always tell <u>me</u> so.

FRED

What of that, my dear? His wealth is of no use to him. He doesn't even make himself comfortable with it.

MARY

I have no patience with him.

FRED

Oh, I have! I'm sorry for him. I couldn't be angry with him if I tried. Who suffers by his ill whims? Himself, always. Here, he takes it into his head to dislike us, and won't come to dine with us. What's the consequence? (*Mischievously*) He doesn't miss much of a dinner!

ALL
Ohhh!

MARY
Indeed, I think he misses a very good dinner!

ALL
(*In mixed unison.*)
And so, say I! And so, say I!

MARY
Do go on, Fred. (*To the others.*) He never finishes what he begins to say. He's such a silly fellow!

FRED
I was only going to say that by <u>not</u> making merry with us, he loses pleasanter company that he can find in his own thoughts or his dusty old chambers. He may rail at Christmas 'til he dies, but I intend to invite him every year, whether he likes it or not. –I defy him! By George, I think I shook him yesterday!

MARY
What happened?

FRED
He called Christmas a "Humbug," as I live! And I countered by wishing him a Merry Christmas!

(*They ALL laugh, and other laughter is heard around the stage. The lights come up on the CRATCHIT FAMILY, and they begin to sing.*)

CRATCHIT FAMILY
(*Singing verse 1 of "Christmas is Coming"*)

Christmas is coming
The geese are getting fat.

Would you please put a penny,
In the old man's hat.
A ha' penny will do.
If you haven't got a ha' penny,
Then God bless you.

MRS. CRATCHIT

Shh! Shhh! Bob, will you do the honors?

CRATCHIT

Delight, my dears!

MRS. CRATCHIT

Children. Ready?

(The FAMILY *sings verse 2 of "Christmas is Coming"*)

Christmas is coming,
The season of good cheer.
Let's all sing a carol,
For the brand New Year.
If you haven't got a carol,
A jolly song will do.
If you haven't got a jolly song,
Then God bless you.

CRATCHIT

A toast to Mr. Scrooge! I give you Mr. Scrooge, the founder of the feast!

FRED

To Uncle Scrooge!

MRS. CRATCHIT

The founder of the feast indeed! I wish I had him here. I'd give him a piece of my mind to feast upon, and I hope he'd have a good appetite for it!

CRATCHIT

My dear, Christmas Day.

MRS. CRATCHIT

Well!

FRED

He has given us plenty of merriment this day, I'm sure. And it would be ungrateful not to drink to his health. And so I say, to Uncle Scrooge!

MRS. CRATCHIT

I'll drink his health for your sake!

FRED

A Merry Christmas and a Happy New Year to the old boy!

ALL

Joy have they that make good cheer!

SCROOGE

Joy have they that make good cheer.

(*The figures of* FRED's PARTY *and the* CRATCHITS *now vanish into the darkness.* SCROOGE *realizes that he is alone.*)

Don't go! Don't - don't - don't go! Not yet. It's too soon! One moment more. One little moment more!

CHRISTMAS PRESENT

No more! My friend, the time draws nigh when Christmas present must cease to be

SCROOGE

Are spirits' lives so short?

CHRISTMAS PRESENT

My life upon this globe is very brief. It ends tonight.

SCROOGE

Tonight!

CHRISTMAS PRESENT

At the strike of the hour! But before I go, you must behold the darkling shapes of two forgotten shadows: Want and Ignorance.

> (*The figures of* WANT *and* IGNORANCE *begin to emerge from* CHRISTMAS PRESENT'S *cloak.*)

Look here!

> (HE *brings out two wretched, abject, pathetic children,* WANT *and* IGNORANCE. THEY *cling to the outside of his garment.*)

O man! Look here. Look, look down here. Look upon them. Where graceful youth should fill their features out and touch them with its freshest tints, a stale and shriveled hand has pinched and twisted them and pulled them into shreds. Where angels might have sat enthroned, devils lurk and menace.

SCROOGE

Spirit, are they yours?

CHRISTMAS PRESENT

"Are there no prisons? Are there no workhouses?"

(HIS *voice echoes on the previous two questions.*)
Mark me! From every seed of evil in that boy, a field of ruin shall grow that shall be gathered in and garnered up and sown again in many places, 'til all the earth is overrun with bitter strife. They are the growth of man's indifference.

(CHRISTMAS PRESENT *exits as the clock chimes. The ghost of* CHRISTMAS FUTURE *enters. His face is invisible within his hood.*)

SCROOGE

I know you. You are the spirit whose coming I dread the most. Ghost of the Future! Will you not speak to me?

(CHRISTMAS FUTURE *remains silent.*)
Lead on, Spirit, lead on.

(*The shadowy followers of* CHRISTMAS FUTURE *begin to reveal themselves as* BUSINESSMEN, *in dark winter coats, hats, and scarves.* THEY *enter in pairs from opposite sides of the stage. Their conversations begin slowly, as out of a dream and from a distance at first.* THEY *begin slowly.* SCROOGE *and* CHRISTMAS FUTURE *look down upon them.*)

FIRST BUSINESSMAN

Well, Old Scratch has got his own at last?

(THEY *laugh, lifelessly.*)

SECOND BUSINESSMAN

So, I see. Cold, isn't it?

FIRST BUSINESSMAN

Seasonable for Christmastime.

ALL BUSINESSMEN
(*Randomly, hollowly*)

Good morning!

THIRD BUSINESSMAN

Well, I don't know much about it, either way. I only know he's dead.

FOURTH BUSINESSMAN

When did he die?

THIRD BUSINESSMAN

Last night, I believe.

SECOND BUSINESSMAN

Why, what was the matter with him? I thought he'd never die.

(*Low laughter from all.*)

THIRD BUSINESSMAN
(*Yawning*)

God knows.

(ALL BUSINESSMEN *yawn*)

FOURTH BUSINESSMAN

What's he done with his money?

THIRD BUSINESSMAN

I haven't heard.

FIRST BUSINESSMAN

He hasn't left it to me. That's all I know.

(THEY *all laugh*)

THIRD BUSINESSMAN

It's likely to be a very cheap funeral, for, upon my life, I don't know of anybody to go to it.

FOURTH BUSINESSMAN
I don't mind going if lunch is provided.

SECOND BUSINESSMAN
I'll offer to go if anybody else will.

FOURTH BUSINESSMAN
Come to think of it, I'm not sure I wasn't his most particular friend. We used to stop and speak whenever we met.

THIRD BUSINESSMAN
Well, I am the most disinterested amongst you all; for I never go to funerals, and I never eat lunch.

(EACH *says* "Hum" *in succession.*)

FIRST BUSINESSMAN
I say, is it too early to stop by the Pub for a pint?

SECOND BUSINESSMAN
How about the Celt, it's closer?

THIRD BUSINESSMAN
Bye., Bye ...

(EACH *says* "Bye, Bye" *as they exit severally.*)

SCROOGE
Who was this man? Is there no one in the city who grieves for him?

(CHRISTMAS FUTURE *remains silent. The figures of* MRS. DILBER, *the laundress;* MRS FILCHER, *the chairwoman; and the* UNDERTAKER'S BOY *begin to manifest themselves in SCROOGE'S chamber.* OLD JOE, *the fence, surprises them from behind the curtains.*)

DILBER
Look here, Old Joe. Fancy meeting you here.

OLD JOE

We couldn't have met in a better place. Come into the parlor my dears, show me what you've stolen, and I'll let you know the value of it.

BOY

I'll show my lot first.

OLD JOE

What have we here from the undertaker's boy? Not worth much. Five shillings.

BOY

Five shillings!

OLD JOE

You ask for another penny, and I'll knock off half a crown. Who's next?

DILBER

It's me next!

OLD JOE

I always give too much to the ladies.

DILBER

A Lady!

OLD JOE

It's a weakness of mine and that's the way I ruin myself. Five Shillings.

DILBER

Five shillings!

FILCHER
(*Laughs at* DILBER *and pushers her aside*)

Here's mine. Wait! Here's something else for me!

(FILCHER *leaps onto the bed and grasps the bed curtains.*)

OLD JOE

What are you doing?

DILBER

What's she up to?

FILCHER

The bed curtains!

OLD JOE

Oh, Mrs. Filcher, you were born to make your fortune and that's fact!

(DILBER *clambers onto the bed and pulls off the blanket.*)

DILBER

Then this is for me!

FILCHER & BOY

His blanket?

DILBER

What does it look like? He ain't likely to catch cold without it.

FILCHER

Here! Give it to me!

DILBER

You got the bed curtains, didn't you?

(THEY *struggle with the blanket.* FILCHER *falls, releasing the blanket.* DILBER *starts to leave with it.*)

FILCHER

Where's she going?

OLD JOE

What do you think we could get for the corpse? No! He's mine.

(THEY *all exit*)

SCROOGE
Spirit, I see, I see. The case of this unhappy man might be my own. Oh, let us leave this fearful chamber. I am afraid. O spirit, let us go.

(CHRISTMAS FUTURE *points at the house.*)

SCROOGE
I cannot bear to look upon him. Show me that sympathy and tender grieving still abide, or this scene will forever haunt me.

(MUSIC: "What Child Is This." VIOLINIST *leads the funeral procession, followed by 2 pall bearers carrying the casket of Tiny Tim. Following is* Mr. & Mrs. CRATCHIT *comforting each other and the* CHILDREN *follow behind them. All are weeping.*)

CRATCHIT
He's gone. He's gone!

(CRATCHIT *puts the crutch on top of the casket and returns to* Mrs. CRATCHIT. *The procession continues to the cemetery. The family goes home.*)

MARTHA
(*Reading from the Bible*)
"He called a little child to Him and took him in His arms and stood among them and said."

PETER
(*Taking the Bible from* MARTHA)
"A child like this is the greatest in the kingdom of Heaven. ... Whosoever shall receive one such little child in my name receiveth me." (*He looks up from the book*) Our Savior loved all children.

MRS. CRATCHIT
(*Looking in from the black shroud on which she has been sewing.*)
Thank you, children. That was very lovely. (*Weeps*) I won't show these tears to your father when he comes home. i expect him soon.

PETER
I think he walks a little slower than he used to, these last few evenings, Mother.

MRS. CRATCHIT
Why, I have known him to walk very fast, even with Tiny Tim upon his shoulders. Very fast indeed.

PETER
And so, have I.

CHILDREN
(*Said in random order*)

And so, have I.

MRS. CRATCHIT
But he was very light to carry. (*Hearing a footstep.*) There's your father now!

(CRATCHIT *enters, and the* CHILDREN *gather around him.*)

BELINDA
Don't mind it, Father. Don't be grieved.

CRATCHIT
Never fear. I'm feeling fine after my walk. I wish you could have gone. It would have done you good to see how pleasant a place it is. Next time, we'll all go. You'll see it often. I promised Tiny Tim we would walk there on a Sunday. My little child. My little Tim. (HE *bursts into tears.*) Sorry, my dears.

(*The* CRATCHITS *exit and* CHRISTMAS FUTURE *begins to move again.*)

SCROOGE
Spirit of the Future, answer me one question; are these the shadows of things that will be-or are they but shadows of things that <u>may</u> be?

(CHRISTMAS FUTURE *remains silent.*)
Can any of this be changed?

(CHRISTMAS FUTURE *points DS, away from* SCROOGE. SCROOGE *looks around.*)
What wretched place is this? (*looking around*) A churchyard, filled with graves and overrun with weeds. (*To* CHRISTMAS FUTURE) Why do you bring me here?

(CHRISTMAS FUTURE *continues to point to the place where a gravestone has slowly begun to emerge from the darkness* SCROOGE *looks at the stone.*)

What forgotten soul rots here? (HE *looks closer and kneels*) What name is this? O, "Ebenezer Scrooge," No spirit. No. No. Spirit, hear me! I am not the man I was. I will not be that man. (HE reaches towards CHRISTMAS

FUTURE) If you assure me that I may yet change these shadows you have shown me by an altered life, I will honor Christmas in my heart and try to keep it all through the year. O tell me that I may wipe away the writing on this stone.

> (HE *puts his head in his hands and weeps.* CHRISTMAS FUTURE *exits. As he does so, Silence.* SCROOGE *is alone.* HE *begins to come to his senses but speaks as if he were still partly in a dream.*)

SCROOGE

I will live in the past, the present, and the future. The spirits of all three shall strive within me. All three alive!

> (*The word "alive" cuts through his dream speech, and* HE *becomes fully conscious once more.*)

That chair–my own! This room–my own room!

> (HE *regards his hand and begins to move his fingers in the growing realization that he is indeed alive.*)

I am alive! Oh, Jacob Marley, I am alive! ALIVE! Heaven and the Christmastime be praised! I say it on my knees. I don't know what to do. I am as giddy as a drunken man! I am as light as a feather! I am as merry as a schoolboy!

> (HE *laughs*)

I love Christmas! A Merry Christmas to everybody! A Happy New Year to all the world!

> (HE *gets out his first big laugh, discovers how pleasant it feels, and experiments with other laughs more elegant, more intricate, louder.*)

I don't know what time it is. I don't know what day it is. I don't know anything. I'm quite a baby. Never mind. I don't care. I'd rather be a baby! Hallo! Whoop! Hallo there!

> (*HE has moved his chair and now stands on it, looking outside. Bells have begun to peal, and he hears them for the first time.*)

O glorious! Glorious!

(*He calls out to a young* BOY *passing by*)

Hallo there!

BOY

Hallo!

SCROOGE

What's today?

BOY

What?

SCROOGE

What's today, my fine fellow?

BOY

Today? Why, Christmas Day!

SCROOGE

It's Christmas Day! *(to himself)* I haven't missed it! The spirits have done it all in one night! Hallo, my fine fellow!

BOY

Hallo!

SCROOGE

Do you know the poultry shop on the next street? The one at the corner?

BOY

I should hope I do.

SCROOGE

An intelligent boy! A remarkable boy! Do you know whether they've sold the prize turkey that was hanging up there? The BIG one.

BOY

The one as big as me?

SCROOGE

What a delightful boy! It's a pleasure to talk to you, my lad! See if it's still there.

BOY
(*Looking*)

It's hanging there now.

SCROOGE

Is it? Go and buy it!

BOY

You're joking!

SCROOGE

No. No. I am in earnest. Go and buy it. (HE *tosses a purse to the* BOY.) Bring it here, and I'll show you where to take it. I'll give you a shilling. Come back in less than five minutes and I'll give you half a crown!

BOY

I'll be back as quick as a shot! (HE *runs off*)

SCROOGE

I'll send it to Bob Cratchit's! Why, it's twice the size of Tiny Tim. Won't they be surprised! I have places to go, people to see and things to do. I love Christmas!

(HE *puts on his outdoor clothes and moves outside.* HE *stops, turns and talks to the door knocker that once held Marley's face.*)

Oh, Jacob Marley, I'm alive! Human welfare is now my business. Charity, mercy, and benevolence will be my business. Merry Christmas, Jacob. A very merry Christmas to you! (HE *breathes deeply*) No fog. No mist. Clear, bright, jovial, stirring, cold. Golden sunlight, heavenly sky, sweet fresh air, merry bells! To be alive! O glorious, glorious!

(*The* BOY *appears with the turkey*)

Oh, there you are, my fine fellow! Follow me. I'll show you where to take it.

(SCROOGE b*egins his glorious walk greeting people along the way with joy.* MUSIC *played:* "God Rest Ye, Merry Gentleman." *Amidst* CAROLERS *and the* VIOLINIST, HE *encounters the two* CHARITABLE GENTLEMEN *at the front of the stage.*)

My dear sirs! How do you do? A Merry Christmas to you, sirs!

FIRST GENTLEMAN
Mr. Scrooge?!

SCROOGE
Yes, that's my name, and I fear it may not be pleasant to you. Allow me to ask your pardon, and will you have the goodness to put me down for . . . (HE *whispers in the* FIRST CHARITABLE GENTLEMAN'S *ear.*)

FIRST GENTLEMAN
Lord bless me! My dear Mr. Scrooge, are you serious?

(SCROOGE *whispers to the* SECOND GENTLEMAN, a*nd then closes his gaping mouth.*)

SCROOGE
Not a farthing less, if you please. A great many back payments are included, I assure you. Will you do me that favor?

SECOND GENTLEMAN
My dear sir, I don't know what to say-

SCROOGE
Don't say anything, please. Will you come and see me?

FIRST & SECOND GENTLEMEN
We will.

(THEY *exit.* SCROOGE *stops to greet* FRED *and* MARY.)

SCROOGE
Fred!

FRED
Why, bless me soul! Who's this?

SCROOGE
It's I, your Uncle Scrooge. I'm coming to dinner! Will you let me in, Fred?

FRED
Let you in! I'd carry you there myself if I could.

SCROOGE
(*To* MARY)
Can you forgive an old fool?

(MARY *nods.* SCROOGE *embraces* FRED *and* MARY *who exit.*)

SCROOGE
(*Calling back*)
Oh, and we'll play a game of "Yes and No."

(SCROOGE *goes to his office*)

DICKENS
Wonderful happiness! Wonderful Happiness! Oh! But he was early at the office the next morning. If he could only be there first and catch Bob Cratchit coming late! That was the thing he'd set his heart upon. And he did it. Yes, he did! Cratchit was full eighteen and a half minutes late.

(CRATCHIT *enters warily.*)

SCROOGE
Hallo! What do you mean by coming here this time of day?

CRATCHIT
I'm very sorry, sir. I am behind my time.

SCROOGE
You are? Yes, I think you are.

CRATCHIT

It's only once a year, sir. It shall not be repeated. I was making rather merry yesterday.

SCROOGE

How, I'll tell you what, my friend. I am not going to stand for this sort of thing any longer. And therefore—and therefore— *(pause)* I am about to raise your salary. *(SCROOGE laughs)* A Merry Christmas, Bob. A merrier Christmas, Bob, my good fellow. Make up the fires and get yourself another scuttle of coal before you dot another "i," Bob Cratchit.

(*The* ENTIRE COMPANY *cheers*.)

DICKENS

Scrooge was better than his word. He did it all, and infinitely more. And to Tiny Tim who did not die, he was a second father. He became as good a friend, as good a master, and as good a man as the good old city knew or any good old city in the good old world. Some people laughed to see the alteration in him, but he let them laugh and little heeded them. For he was wise enough to know that nothing good ever happens on this globe without some people having their fill of laughter at the outset. His own heart laughed, and that was enough for him. And it was always said of him that he knew how to keep Christmas well if any man on earth did. And may that truly be said of us and all of us. And so, as Tiny Tim observed

(DICKENS *closes the book*)

TINY TIM
"God bless us, everyone."

(MUSIC: "We Wish You a Merry Christmas.")

DICKENS
Everyone please, sing along with us.

ALL

(The VIOLINIST *plays the final chorus and it is sung by* EVERYONE, *including the audience.)*
We wish you a Merry Christmas,
We wish you a Merry Christmas,
We wish you a Merry Christmas and a Happy New Year.
Good tidings we bring to you and your kin,
We wish you a Merry Christmas and a Happy New Year.

THE END.

Special Thanks to the cast members of the 2023 *A Christmas Carol* who served as models for the illustrations

(by appearance in play)

Ebenezer Scrooge	Dale G. Gutt
Bob Cratchit	Dennis Ryazanov
Fred	Dylan K. Haney
Ghost of Jacob Marley	John Baker
Young Scrooge	Brett Lee
Belle Cousins	Summer Austin
Mr. Fezziwig	James Dorrell
Mrs. Fezziwig	Kelly Baxter
Dancer at Fezziwig party	Merrek Maloney
Ghost of Christmas Present	Justice Williams
Waifs (Want & Ignorance)	Asher and Barrett Dougherty
Tiny Tim	Owen Poole
Ghost of Christmas Past	Teresa Miller